The Darkness Unveiled

Investigating the Hidden World

By: Randy Tatum

THE DARKNESS UNVEILED: INVESTIGATING THE HIDDEN WORLD
Copyright © 2018 by Randy Tatum

All rights reserved.
No part of this publication may be reproduced or distributed in any form or by any means.

Cover Art by: Randy Tatum
Edited by: Randy Tatum
Pictures in book: Melissa Calvert of Light of Luna Photography

ISBN-13: 978-1726036245
ISBN-10: 1726036243

Printed in the U.S.A.

Contents

Introduction	7
The Start	10
Old Bryce (Jemison Building)	14
Woodruff-Fontaine	31
Sardis	41
Cemeteries	54
Orbs	65
Effects from Hunting	69
Theories	73
Something Good	80
Conclusion	83
Acknowledgements	89

"If I got rid of my demons, I'd lose my angels"
Tennessee Williams

Introduction

There is a world that exists that no one can explain. The reception of this realm is full of laughs and scoffs. People just have a difficult time believing something that is not gifted to them in plain sight. This is why I believe people have slowly become less and less religious—if God doesn't appear before us and slap us in the face, he doesn't exist right? But maybe there is a reality that surrounds us that we take for granted everyday. Maybe what is before our very eyes is an incomplete reality. It would be accurate to say what we know as reality is only a speck in the array of matter around us.

When we were young we were told there is a Santa Claus, and we believed it without question. The neighborhood kids told us that there were monsters under our bed and to beware walking near the woods, because Goatman was going to come out and grab you up to eat you, and we trembled. The amount of mythology that surrounded us our entire life became a seed that in our adult years produced doubt among us all. To find out that Santa Claus wasn't real, Goatman really wasn't going to ever come out and eat you, or the monsters under our bed were nothing but smelly gym socks we had forgotten to put in the hamper for Mom to wash, really threw our minds into a whirlwind of disbelief. If all of these were fiction, what else had we been lied to about our entire life?

This isn't a religious book. I'm not here to convert you, although I do completely believe in God as well as demons. This book's purpose is to make you aware of a reality that is unequivocally alive and breathing amongst us every day. What once was speculation and by most perceived as fantasy, spirits are a proven reality. There is room for speculation of what these said spirits are or why they are here, but the fact that they exist can no longer be challenged.

When I started ghost hunting, I had no idea what to expect. I was always open to the idea of there being ghosts, and in a sense it was sort of wishful thinking, being a kid who absolutely adored horror movies. But when I really got immersed into ghost hunting, I really began to realize that as humans we know very little. There are things at work behind the scenes that we take for granted simply because they aren't staring us in the face (at least we can't see them staring us in the face.)

In this book, I plan to present you with a lot of the evidence that my crew and I obtained over the few years we embarked on the adventure of ghost hunting. I want to offer you a look into a realm that we once believed was just some scary film we saw. This book may provide insight to some; to others it may present more questions than answers. The important thing is that we do eventually come to insight or questioning. When we remain stagnant, not willing to find out the mysteries of the universe, we lose our sense of purpose. If these things exist—which I assure you they do—there must be a reason. To look at this evidence and just plainly say "ah, that's cool" and then go no further with it, is to deny yourself the answers to the mystery of why we are all here. If life is really nothing and our existence is really meaningless, why would things exist beyond what we can see?

I hope that this book provides a spiritual awareness. Even if it produces fear, I believe it is very important that we all become and remain spiritually aware. If spirits are active in our every day life or if spirits can influence our every day life, we need to know this. If you are a believer in the paranormal, I hope that this book becomes a reminder; if you are a skeptic, I hope you trust that our experiences are true and it turns you into a believer. From there, I hope you dig deeper to determine what you really believe in, because although some don't think so, what we believe in is crucial to life itself. If we go our entire life an agnostic with anything whether it is religion, politics, finances or anything really, our lives have really become anything but useful, and everything we do is truly in vain. I hope this book, beyond just a bunch of stories and evidence of the paranormal, strikes a chord in every person's brain to think far beyond what we know as reality. The hidden darkness among us will soon be unveiled for all to see.

The Start

I was working on writing one of my books in Starbucks, sipping my coffee, deeply immersed in the story I was telling, when a young guy with long hair, glasses and a black band T-shirt sat in the chair next to me. "Do you mind if I ask you a question? I'm kind of doing research." I was caught a little off guard, having to break from the storyline in my head. "Huh?" is what probably came out of my mouth, so he repeated himself. I agreed, although wondered if I was being pranked or trolled in some way. He had a notepad in his hand and a pen in the other, prepared to write my response.

"Have you ever had a paranormal experience?" He asked.

"What exactly kind of paranormal are you talking about?" I asked, still adjusting from the transfer from fictitious writing to real life.

"Anything really. Either ghosts, aliens, just anything that stands out from the norm."

I racked my brain, thinking if I had ever seen or heard anything. After a few moments, I finally remembered that I had seen a UFO once when I was in Las Vegas. Aside from that nothing else came to mind. The guy wrote down my experience and then he started back in making sure there wasn't something I had forgotten from my past. Nothing came to mind. So, I turned it back to him. "Are you writing a book? Have you had anything paranormal happen?" He had more than just a reply for me; he had proof.

The Darkness Unveiled: Investigating the Hidden World

We finally had exchanged names, and Chance told me to follow him out onto the patio of Starbucks. "It's too loud in there. It's a little better out here to hear," he said to me. I still had no idea what we were going out to listen to.

Chance reached into his pocket and pulled out just a small digital recorder. He told me that his girlfriend's parents own a house that was soon to be rented out or sold to someone else. It was empty at this moment. He told me about a former family that had lived there, and the mother had hung herself in a closet. I knew exactly which house he was talking about. It was a beautiful house—very similar to a young girl's dollhouse, only life-size. My sister had told me the story of the woman before, because she actually knew the sons who lived there. So, I was well aware of the house. Chance proceeded to tell me that he and his girlfriend went into the house to do an EVP (Electronic Voice Phenomenon) recording and that he had captured a voice. Electronic Voice Phenomenon is common in ghost hunting. EVPs are obtained by using a digital recorder to record ghosts speaking. Voices that aren't audible to the human ear will frequently manifest on these recorders.

I've kind of always believed in the paranormal, but I never had an experience with any kind of spirits. When he said this I was certainly open-minded to it. Although I didn't really know Chance, his face was authentic. I had no doubt in my mind that I may actually really hear a real ghost on the audio. My assumptions didn't let me down.

He pressed play, and I heard his voice sound off from the recorder. "Miss Patti, are you hear with us today?" There was a pause, but then from the depths of the silence, a muffled voice sounded, **"I am."** I couldn't believe my ears. I had to hear it again. The same voice sounded again with every listen, 'I am.' Why 'Miss Patti' was still in the house or who else might have been there pretending to be Miss Patti, I wasn't sure, nor did I really care at that moment. I just finally knew that there was a way to communicate with things that people laughed off or had told me forever was a myth. Completely hooked and dumbfounded, I talked to Chance for several hours, and in just those few hours, we became friends.

Several Starbucks meetings later, Chance and I had formed a pretty solid friendship, which would eventually send us down a path into the unknown. We both agreed that we should start a ghost hunting team. We had nothing better to do than to spend all of our time smelling coffee and drooling over our books or computers. After discussing it for several minutes, Chance and I decided that it would need to be more than just us two. We would at least need a third person for a solid team. We could start out small and bring others into the mix later, which is precisely what we did. Chance suggested a friend who was also interested in the paranormal as well as photography. She wound up being a mutual friend of mine in this small world we fell into. So, we immediately called up Melissa. She was instantly onboard, and we began our first investigations.

The Darkness Unveiled: Investigating the Hidden World

With every investigation, the three of us were sucked in more and more. Sometimes we obtained no evidence, sometimes numerous amounts of evidence. The hunt was a thrill. The search was addicting. Figuring out where we would go next was constantly on the agenda. Revisiting places that were clearly haunted became a pastime. For almost a year, nearly 90% of our weekends were filled with ghost hunts, and it continued years after. This journey created a lot of questions that we were eager to dive into and dissect.

OLD BRYCE (JEMISON BUILDING)

Background of Jemison Building (Old Bryce)

The halls of trees that usher guests that visit Old Bryce might cause confusion, creating an illusion that the path may actually lead to nowhere. Suddenly after being surrounded and veiled by trees, following nothing but a craggy, concrete path, a clearing opens up and there it appears—massive, rickety and hauntingly desolate.

The Jemison Building, which has been branded Old Bryce, was built in the 1939. It was opened as a means of giving the mentally ill an alternative to the treatment they were being given at the main Bryce Hospital. At Old Bryce, which being that it was an addition to the original Bryce, was really "New Bryce", the patients were given jobs as a form of therapy. Rather than being cooped up all day watching TV or simply just staring at the walls, the patients were given jobs that reflected everyday life. It was a sort of moral therapy that didn't include restraints, however included real interaction and therapeutic work. The Jemison building acted somewhat as a dormitory that was close to the farmland where they worked.

In the 1970s a judge ruled that the work these patients were doing had to be paid labor if it was going to continue. Unfortunately, the hospital couldn't afford to pay the patients, so all of the farming activities had to be purged, and the patients were sent back into the secure areas of the hospital. They were only able to go outside periodically and were left with few if any activities, which may have had a negative affect on the patients.

Our Old Bryce Investigation

My heart hammered in my throat that day. Swallowing had become a faint memory of permitted bodily functions. What we heard that day, what we experienced would forever change my perception of the reality we all take for granted—the reality that is veiled before us. It's the reality we all trudge by daily with no acknowledgement, the reality we descry momentarily only to dismiss it as something else. Only a slap in the face, a knife to the stomach, a handheld, physical experience could relieve us any further disputes of the reality before us.

The night was cool and calm. The moon was out, and there was a slight breeze in the air. We had arrived at Bryce Mental Institution in Tuscaloosa, Alabama around eight o'clock, just after sundown. Our crew, which was the four of us on this particular day, was in full armor, ready for whatever would come our way—or so we thought. We were fresh ghost hunters with little experimental equipment. With only my video camera, a photography camera, a digital recorder and our brave shells, we walked up the rugged path that they used to call a driveway. As we quietly kicked up dirt and stray gravel, the trees above gnarled their bony fingers above us, allowing slight patterns of the moon's glow to form ghostly images at our feet.

We were forced to park a quarter of a mile away from the actual facility, because we were told the town police periodically patrolled the area for trespassing kids that wished to spray graffiti or smash the walls in the derelict design. We weren't welcome there in more ways than one. The most important thing was that we not go to jail that night.

This wasn't the first time we had been to what has been called Bryce Mental Institution. A friend made us aware of the place about a year before this investigation, and we immediately fell in love. The

The Darkness Unveiled: Investigating the Hidden World

building is massive with three floors as well as a basement. Looking at it, you'd think it had been forgotten, but to thrill seekers and adventurers it has remained a playground of wonder.

As we got closer, ignoring the "Posted: No Trespassing" sign, Bryce emerged through the trees glowing like a baby being birthed. Many of the windows were missing or busted out. The door to the front was hanging on one hinge. Debris was everywhere: electrical wire that had been stripped, sheetrock, busted concrete—it was a beautiful disaster. We stood outside for a number of minutes taking pictures and just marveling at the building that was about to swallow us whole.

Chance, Melissa, Leah and I walked in hearing the debris crunch beneath our feet. We took light steps, not knowing if we might walk up on a crazed homeless person or some of those graffiti artists. So far we had witnessed neither, only the quietness and the eerie presence of this entity we called a building.

As we walked through the front door, hoping the last hinge wouldn't snap and fall on us, the room opened up into a sort of lobby. Directly ahead stood a staircase covered in debris, which made it inaccessible to us. Directly below, a door that led into a large room. We looked to the right, which possessed a long corridor that looked literally destroyed; even the ceiling seemed to be caving in down this particular hall. Looking left, we saw what seemed to be a safe corridor that had several small rooms to search along the way. Our first plan was to map out the place, then begin our investigation.

We took small steps, looking down occasionally as to not step on nails or trip over anything. Making our way down the hallway, it was still quiet besides our heavy breathing and the crunch beneath our feet. The only other sound was the crickets outside. I looked in the first room we came to and there was a bathtub with a chair seated right beside it. I imagined decades before the orderlies bathing the patients. It gave me chills.

Interrupting my thoughts, all of a sudden, we heard a loud repetitive sound that sounded as if air was being let out of a tire. Wide eyed and frozen, I looked at Chance. He had the same look of fear on his face. Curious what it could be we looked in the room. The room was barely the size of a closet. No one was in there, but lying on the ground was **an aerosol spray can steadily spraying out air**. We couldn't believe our eyes. Absolutely no one was in the room. Finally, either the can ran out of air or whatever was spraying it decided to move on. Our hearts were beating fast in our chests, but we still moved on.

Not even five steps later, we get to a room just across the hall from the aerosol can. The room is just before a doorway that opens up into a large room that may have been a recreational room or some sort of common room. We glanced in the room, and walked on, anxious to get to the common room and see the rest of the building. Before we could walk through the doorway we heard **loud beating on the walls of the room**. We could see every inch of the room, but absolutely no one was in there. Following close behind the beating, in the recreational room, we heard what sounded like **an old black man's muffled voice.** This was far too overwhelming for us, so a few of us started to run. Chance said "Don't run, don't run" because he was very curious what the sound was, but honestly, I didn't want to find out. The entire group followed. The truth is none of us were brave enough to stick around.

We congregated outside, catching our breath and discussed what the explanation could be other than paranormal. We came to a conclusion that none of them could really be explained except perhaps the voice. Maybe someone was in there. The inside of the building is lit very well by the moonlight. Plenty of windows give light to anything physical that might be in there. We didn't see anything or anyone, so that didn't really make sense either.

Several minutes passed before we made our way back into Bryce. We wanted to give whatever entity was in there a few minutes to calm down. Looking back I wish we had stayed and braved the insanity. When we got back in, everything had calmed down. Nothing was heard. Any moment we thought something might scare us back out, but nothing else of that caliber emerged. The four of us explored the rest of Bryce, seeing the graffiti stained walls at every turn and the wreckage and decay of the walls and bones of the place. It was apparent that sometime in years past homeless people had gathered there for warmth, having several rooms possessing twin-sized mattresses. I assume that as time passed, the constant swarm of hunters and explorers repelled the homeless, and now they were nowhere in sight.

After we did a full run of the house and retrieved a few EVPs we made our way to the basement. Our team decided to try something a little different than we had before. The plan was to sit in the largest room in the basement, shut all the lights out, and just record on our digital recorder. In this session we just sat and asked questions, and for a period just sat there in the quietness. About midway through our session, we started to hear **a rustle across the room.** There was a single high window in the basement, which gave enough light, and now that our eyes were acclimated, we could see almost as if it were daytime. So, we looked at where the rustle was, wondering if we might see a mouse or something to send us jumping up and out, but there was nothing we could see. The rustling began to sound like faint footsteps that seemed to be keeping close to the wall, walking the perimeter. They were getting closer—slowly but edging closer. We only could look at each other in the blue light of the moon, having the wide white of our eyes glowing. The sound was now behind me. It inched closer and closer until I felt it right on the back of my neck. **A cold chill of wind grazed the back of my neck.** At this point, I couldn't take it anymore. With one click, I cut on my Maglight and gasped for air. The chill was gone.

The Darkness Unveiled: Investigating the Hidden World

We had a few other visits to Bryce. My count is four if I can remember correctly. The visits blend a little because of the monotony—not of the experiences, rather the timelines. Our adventures always seemed to start in the same place and end in the same place. One of the experiences was completely a bust. Absolutely nothing happened there except rain. It was only three of us for that experience. This time we were glad no one came with us, because our hype of the place had become a highlight of conversations to any of our friends that had interest or might be skeptical.

Out of the four visits to Tuscaloosa to see this amazing building, two were just fantastic and fruitful (if that's the word for it) experiences. The other experience that I'd like to discuss, to be quite honest I can't remember who all was exactly with us. As I said before, the experiences seem to blur as one in my mind. I could've simply written this as one complete experience, but I plan to be as honest and as accurate as I can possibly be. So, with that being said, I will speak of the two that were almost entirely at every investigation I went on: Chance and Melissa (the three of us really being THE team). Everyone else that joined us sporadically came along—some several times, some seldom. I digress. So, for the sake of argument it was Chance, Mel, and I (as well as one or two more people).

This particular investigation, although active, certainly didn't have the activity of the previous investigation. However, the significance and validity overshadow our most active investigation. The reason I say this is because we actually captured some chilling things on video! Yes, that's right, you can actually visit YouTube and find our most significant finds this particular investigation. (**Just search for "Bryce Mental Institution sounds caught on tape," and it should be the first video to pop up**).

The timeline is similar to the first story, only the same malevolent spirits didn't greet us immediately to send us out the door with our tails between our legs. This would've been our third visit to Old Bryce—the first being an introductory, the second being the insanity as discussed before. So, this time, although still terrified deep down that we might have another experience as before, we seemed to be warming up to the place. Everything was familiar to us. The place seemed to be more like home to us than before, and our trepidation was blanketed; I'll admit, the blanket was probably thin, but a blanket covered us nonetheless.

We took the same path as before, hoping to stir up the same spirits we had before. So, far it hadn't worked. Our group had already made it into the common room without anything happening. That wouldn't last long, this we were sure of. Getting through the common room, we walked through a door that opened up to a room that was very rectangular. The length was probably four or five times its width, giving it the appearance of a hallway rather than a room. It's unclear to me exactly what the room was used for. Perhaps it was just a continuation of the common room. This seemed like a fine place to collect some audio. So, I started up my camera, and Chance started his digital recorder. Melissa was snapping pictures here and there. Generally, we tend to collect EVPs from anywhere, whether from a feeling or we just feel like its time for one. I can't say that we had some feeling at the time, but we ended up choosing the right area.

The camera was rolling; the red light on Chance's audio recorder was glowing. Then, we clicked the buttons on our flashlights, and there we were in the dark with only the faint color of the moonlight streaming in.

Chance: "Could you please tell us your name?"
    Silence
Chance: "Could you tell us what you are doing here?"
    Silence
Chance: "Are you dead?"
    Silence
Chance: "What year is it?"
    Silence
Chance: "Could you tell us the year in which you died?"

At that moment you could hear **feet running across the room**. It sounded as if it were bare feet running across a puddle in a Doppler Effect fashion—first starting loud and fading away as if whoever it was ran out of the room. It was clearly in the room with us. My hair stood straight up. I cut on my flashlight to see if I could see anyone or anything; there was nothing or no one.

Chance: "Could you do that again? Can you please make the noise that you just made?"

Ambient noise outside.

Chance: "We are not here to disturb you, we are just curious about who you are and why you are here. We mean you no disrespect."

Silence

Chance: "We appreciate your time tonight. If there is anything you'd like to say, say it now."

Silence

We reviewed the audio we recorded in that room, and nothing other than the footsteps were discovered, but whatever was there was certainly active enough to manifest itself physically rather than electronically, which for us is a very unusual thing.

Soon after, we ventured to the second floor. The second floor was a place we hadn't spent a lot of time the first two times we had visited Bryce. The third floor looked as if it had been burned and didn't seem very safe. The second floor wasn't in the greatest shape, but it was sturdy enough for us to check it out. Once up there we came to a room and decide to record some more audio. So, same as before, I started my camera, and Chance started the digital recorder.

Chance: "Can you tell us your name?"

Silence.

Chance: "Can you let us know that you are there?"

Immediately after Chance's question, **something in the room falls.** Startled, we all jump back, my camera shaking like a mad man. Chance is steadily trying to calm us down so we are able to get further audio. We do end up trying to obtain more audio, but we end up getting nothing.

After reviewing all of our audio, which collectively was well over an hour, we found nothing solid or worthy of public exhibition. Although the audio was a bust, the experience was one of the best that we have ever had. We obtained pictures that are certainly worthy of exhibition, video evidence of something paranormal, and the story for all to hear. If you ever make your way to Tuscaloosa, Alabama, I'd like to say you should go check it out, but the truth is you may end up in jail. Old Bryce may be a playground to some, grounds for exploration for others, but to whatever phantom entity is surreptitiously lurking in the shadows, it is its place of unrest—its home for eternity.

The bathtub and chair for orderlies to watch patients bathe.

Room where the aerosol can sprayed at us.

The Darkness Unveiled: Investigating the Hidden World

The hallway we captured the feet running on audio with orbs (likely just dust)

Room I had the chill on my neck.

Randy Tatum

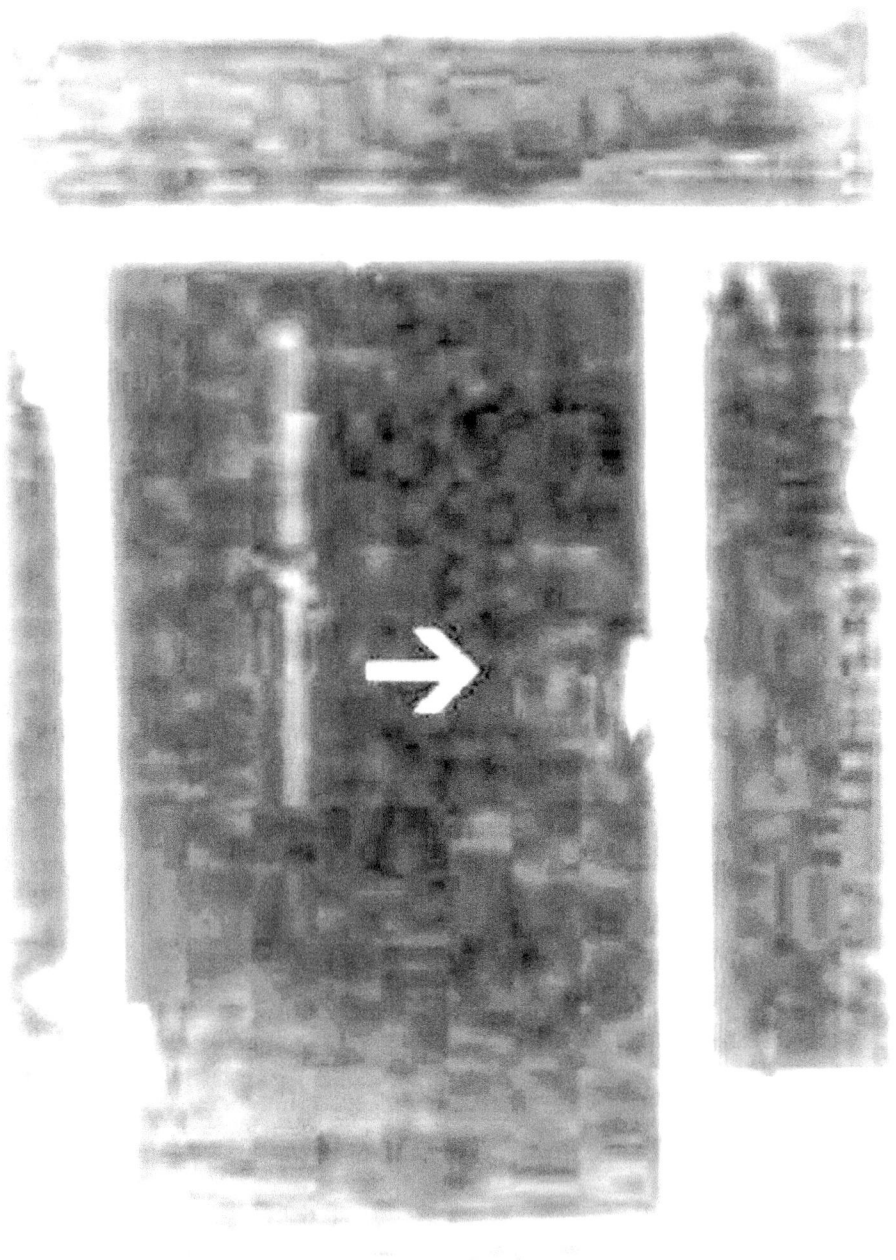

Zoomed in possible Apparition. Difficult to see in black and white

The Darkness Unveiled: Investigating the Hidden World

Zoomed in faces of possible spirits manifested on the floor. (Again, difficult to see in black and white)

Randy Tatum

Face in the bottom right corner of the window looking in at us

**Note: The quality of the photos is poor because in the photos' original formats, the faces and apparitions would be difficult to see, so they had to be edited and enlarged.

WOODRUFF-FONTAINE HOUSE

Background of Woodruff-Fontaine House

Located in Victorian Village, once referred to as "Millionaire's Row" in Memphis, Tennessee, The Woodruff-Fontaine House stands tall, overlooking Adams Ave. The soft ominous glow of the windows anticipates the figures that may shift from room to room. When walking by you can't help but position yourself directly in front to catch a glimpse of this beauty.

Amos Woodruff, a carriage maker, who came to Memphis to grow his carriage business, built the mansion in 1870. He lived there with his family, including one of the most notable residents Mollie Woodruff, his daughter, who is said to still roam the house. He sold his house in 1892 to Noland Fontaine of a very prominent cotton company, which was one of the largest cotton companies in the world. Noland married and had ten children—one of whom also is said to haunt the third floor of the building; his name was Elliot.

Mollie's bedroom also referred to as the "Rose Room" was where she suffered the loss of her newborn baby. Another dark stain on the room was the demise of Mollie's husband Egbert Wooldridge who was said to have either died of pneumonia or staph infection. Although Mollie moved and did not pass away in the house, it is said that her spirit returned there. People have reported impressions on the bed, appearing that someone is lying down. Also, it seems Mollie's temper piques when furniture is moved around; there have been reports of doors slamming and things breaking as well as Mollie's voice in the docent's ears saying "That doesn't go there." Mollie's interactions seem a little more docile than that of Elliot's who is the malevolent spirit of the house. Elliot has pushed docents and guests, and they have also felt as if he was pompously standing right next to them. People have also heard whistling they believe to be Elliot.

Our Woodruff-Fontaine Investigation

Having the privilege of being one of the only ghost hunting crews to have been given complete access to this building unescorted to investigate, we can attest to the activity that is so wildly spoken about by the docents as well as other visitors. Of our three investigations, one visit in particular stands out as giving us one of the most original and interesting audio recordings we have ever had or have ever heard from any other ghost hunting crew. On this particular occasion many other things happened to us as well. It was an investigation that would stand out from many adventures to come.

When we were permitted to enter into the Woodruff-Fontaine house unaccompanied, we were ecstatic. It is a rare occurrence for a team of hunters to be able to enter this house alone to investigate, because there are so many valuable, Victorian age antiques. We were sure to make the most of our visit not knowing if we'd ever be allowed back. Accompanying Chance, Mel, and I were Chance's brother and one of our friends, Eron. We had three hours to try and obtain the most evidence we possibly could.

The docent gave us a brief tour to begin our investigation, noting the 'hotspots' of the house. He shared with us his own encounters with a spirit that is said to wander the house named Elliot. Elliot is supposedly the malevolent spirit of the house that seems to have aggressive tendencies not limited to the excessiveness of trying to push visitors and docents down the stairs. It is said that Elliot mostly resides on the third floor, which ends up being the most active floor of our investigation. Another 'ghostly resident' of the Woodruff Fontaine house is Mollie who seems to mostly stay on the second floor in or near her bedroom. Her room typically stays ten degrees colder than any other room in the house, which may be insulation or some other weather related issue but worth noting nonetheless.

After our brief tour it was off to investigating. By this time we had upped our equipment a little, now using a K-II meter, infrared thermometer, a motion sensor, our typical camera and camcorder and our usual digital recorder. The first thing we wanted to do was to place the motion sensor on the third floor, just incase while we were wandering the rest of the house, Elliot may reveal to us that he is active upstairs. So, Chance and I, in the pitch black, ascended the steps, nervousness tickling the pits of our stomachs. We decided the best approach, for the best, most accurate result was to place the motion sensor at our chest level. This would eliminate the chance of false results due to critters that could be scurrying in the house. So, we placed it on the handrail at the end of the stairs. That was definitely high enough to free us from error or ill results. Before we came back downstairs, Chance and I heard a loud sound that sounded almost like **a single low dog bark,** but it wasn't. You can hear me on the camera audio say, "What was that?" Melissa then called out from downstairs saying that she was walking and it was wood creaking below her feet, however, if you watch the tape back, you can hear the tiny squeak under her feet, but the sound we heard overshadowed it and didn't even seem to be under her feet. We didn't attempt to debunk it in the moment because we thought that it really might have been just someone walking. Although it could have been boards creaking, I'm not entirely convinced.

So, we shrugged off the sound and with the sensor facing the most open section of the upstairs foyer, we descended back down the stairs to the second floor. As we get to the second floor, **the motion sensor immediately starts dinging**. Something or someone had walked by it. Being that no one was in the house but us, our only conclusion was that something ghostly had walked by it, perhaps following us on our descent. We actually did capture this on my video camera that Eron was holding, which shows our precise location when we are going down the stairs. There is no way based on our positioning that it could have been Chance or I who set off the motion sensor. If I had to play devil's advocate, I could argue that maybe the motion sensor had some sort of delay on it that resulted in a delayed detection of us before we went down the stairs. However, this would've been the only time said delayed reaction had occurred when accounting for future investigations. Being that the batteries were brand new and the motion sensor was brand new, such a defect seems to be unlikely.

The noise of the sensor sent us back up to the third floor to see if we could capture any audio. We brought the camera and the recorder up and wandered around. While Eron was recording, **something hit the camcorder** he was holding. This as well was captured and uploaded. You can hear a loud knock on the camera, and then you hear Eron say "What the..." He then explained to us that something had hit the camera and knocked it up. Could he have possibly bumped into something and just not realized it? Sure. However, when he cuts on the light to the camera, you can see that he doesn't seem to be near anything that he might knock into. So, I'm still under the impression that this is certainly supernatural.

Very soon after we were doing something with the camera, maybe changing a battery, Chance was recording on his recorder. He didn't ask a question or provoke at all, he was just recording simply to see if anything manifested. This is when we got one of the best, most clear EVPs we had ever recorded.

"Tears (sigh) eternal (faint laughing)" was what manifested.

With a number of EVPs we have to guess at what they are saying or enhance the sound so great to hear even one word. This particular EVP barely had to be enhanced, and there is no question in our mind that these were the exact words spoken. It was the sound of a male's voice, perhaps the malevolent spirit they call Elliot. Was he trying to tell us that he is sad or in pain now for all eternity? Is he in Hell that is somehow leaking into our own reality here? Is it a demon? It is unclear exactly what he might mean here, but one thing is obvious, this isn't a positive message. And the faint laughter paints an ominous coat on the entire message. I don't pretend to be an expert on these kind of things—no one really is; there is just no way of us knowing for sure what any of this means or where it comes from. I do in fact have my own theories, which I will discuss in another chapter.

Upon review of other EVPs we recorded, we did have a few others, but none as notable as the one discussed above. We had one that said, **"Go back!"** just as I cut on my flashlight. You can hear the click of my flashlight, and almost instantly the voice says, **"Go back!"** Could the spirit have been telling another spirit to 'go back' because lights were being cut on? Maybe they needed to be in a darker area. I'm not really sure, but it certainly wasn't a random EVP. It most definitely was in reference to my Maglight being illuminated. We also obtained an audio recording that said, **"Help!"** We get 'help' and 'hello' fairly often so when we get these, honestly, we aren't very impressed. I'm not sure if 'help' really means help. My personal opinion is that if these were spirits actually reaching out for help, we would eventually know more than we know, but that is simply not the case. I will go into this in slightly more detail in a later chapter. There was another EVP that came from what is known as an intelligent spirit. An intelligent spirit manifests in direct response to questions asked or demands. In this one, Chance said, "Please, make a noise again." The response immediately was clearly **"Okay."**

We are not scientists, nor do we claim to be, but sometimes you just have to try something that is out of the ordinary. Unsure if this would produce any results at all, I had Chance call my cell phone from his. We flipped the receivers, putting the mouthpiece of my phone to the earpiece of his and vice versa. Doing this creates a feedback that we hoped would create a gateway for voices to manifest. Unfortunately this failed to produce any results as far as voices. However, while we did this, we did place the KII meter close by and we did have **a huge spike on it,** and it went all the way to red, which is good evidence of paranormal activity. It's possible that the cell phones alone may have made the meter spike, but it only had that severe of a spike once during the entire session. Maybe it's a coincidence? A noise did happen on the cell phones that had never happened before. Contrasting from the usually feedback was **a loud, distorted—almost alarm sounding** repeatedly. We captured this on video as well, and on video I am heard asking Chance what he did. He said that he didn't do anything. This was the only time this loud distortion had ever happened.

As far as the rest of the house, nothing was as active as the third floor. We may have gotten a feeling here or a feeling there, but no unquestionable evidence that we'd feel comfortable boasting about as infallible. Even Mollie's room was quiet and undisturbed. Although nothing further happened as far as the paranormal goes, I

The Darkness Unveiled: Investigating the Hidden World

did in fact scare worse than I have ever scared on an investigation. I was on the third floor and decided to go up the stairwell leading to the crow's nest of the house. I walked the stairs alone, hearing them creak and moan below my feet. When I finally reached the top, I saw a little girl looking out the crow's nest window dressed in all white. I literally gasped very loud. After I finally caught my breath, I realized that this was a mannequin prop they put up there to creep people out that walked by the house. Hearing my gasping, Chance called up to me to see what happened. By this time, I had made the discovery that it was a mannequin, so I was laughing.

The mannequin that scared me nearly to death (imagine coming up a dark stairwell to this!)

The back of Woodruff-Fontaine House

Possible mist in the mirror (could be a smudge)

SARDIS HOSPITAL

Background of North Panola Hospital

There is actually very little background known about the North Panola Hospital—or as we like to call it Sardis Hospital. It sits up on the hill overlooking the interstate at the Sardis, Mississippi exit. The place is very ominous, projecting sparse illumination by only a few streetlights down the hill and a gas station. Strangely enough, the hospital actually closed around Halloween in the nineties. There are still decorations of paper pumpkins all over the walls. No known major traumatic experience has happened there, however, a hospital is definitely a walkway for spirits to wander aimlessly.

Reports of doors slamming and photos of a shadow that looks like a woman wearing a nurse's cap are among some of the activity that has been reported there. The place is very quiet and dark, but behind the shadows, there is something lurking that I believe to be very sinister. It may be a good thing that all ghost-hunting groups were eventually barred from ever coming back.

Our Investigation of North Panola Hospital

There is something about abandoned hospitals that I find so interesting. The thousands of diverse people that have come in and out for different ailments—some being revived and some never seeing another sunrise ever again—creates a chilling vibe.

Being that the building isn't really that old and freshly closed, this typically wouldn't be an attraction for paranormal teams, however, reports of many strange things happening in there was brought to my attention by a police officer. I lucked up on being able to enter this place. Living within fifty miles of this place, one would think that I might have heard of it or heard some stories about it, but it was sheer luck that I was even made aware of it. I was working at a gun shop for my grandfather. During slow hours, I would get on my laptop and listen as well as look at evidence we had gathered from the weekend before. There were several regulars that would come into the gun shop just to shoot off at the mouth (no pun intended) and gander at guns, never really buying anything.

The Darkness Unveiled: Investigating the Hidden World

While I was on my laptop taking a look at pictures, one of the regulars, a police officer, glanced at my laptop. "What are you looking at?" I explained, waiting for the chuckle that I generally get from people I tell about my ghost hunting ventures. Only his face was pretty serious and demonstrated unmitigated interest. We talked for a few minutes about ghosts and things I had experienced. He blurted out "You should try going to the Sardis Hospital. All kinds of weird things are said to happen there." I was interested, but it didn't seem plausible to gain access. Before I could even ask, he said, "I can hook you up. I know the guy that has the key." He pulled out a pen and wrote down the man's number on a scratch sheet of paper. "He's the chief at the police department that's right beside the hospital. You tell him Jeff gave you his number, and he will set you up."

That weekend I called, and we had our date and time set…

The door was already unlocked for us when we got there. The six of us walked in, immediately met by a gurney. It was quite a welcoming to be greeted with a stretcher that hundreds of people had laid, possibly died on. Walking by it, I imagined the people that might have been on it, covered from head to toe in a white sheet, one toe hanging out at the end with a tag on it, wheels below squeaking as they carried the patient to the morgue just a few hundred feet down the hall. It was all so eerie to fantasize about.

We took the left hallway, flashlights glowing. Several desks and chairs were stacked in corners. There were filing cabinets—

some open, some closed—containing records of former patients. Unlike many places we go in, this hospital was fully intact. There were no busted up walls, no graffiti; the officers that oversaw the place had obviously been doing a good job of surveillance. The stacked chairs and boxes that blocked some doorways reminded me of a barricade you might witness in a zombie film. It seemed like something awful had gone down, and in an attempt to get away quickly, the chairs and debris was pushed tightly against the doors to slow down the attacker.

We finally got to a stairwell. It was either continue upward or find out what else might be downstairs. Before we could continue upstairs, we wanted to double back and see what else the bottom floor had to offer. Walking back through, we saw what looked like a receptionist room with a large window. Just around the corner from that was what looked like a surgery room. It had a large dome-like light suspended in it. Continuing down the corridor we finally came to the room we were most excited about investigating—the morgue. It was a large room, appearing similar to a garage. A dirty mattress lay on the floor. Many stray planks of wood, doors that had been taken off hinges, overhead lights, and a lonely wooden crutch were amongst the debris that was strewn throughout the room. It seemed to have become somewhat of a storage area. We would start here.

We decided since we hadn't explored the entire first floor yet that we would lay the recorder down in the morgue, explore the rest in the meantime, then come back and check it. Taking note of any ambient sounds we might have made that we could mistake on the recorder as paranormal, we wandered the rest of the first floor. After about ten minutes, we came back and collect the recorder. What ended up manifesting on the recorder is one of the most intense, raw inexplicable recordings we have ever had. **A loud, distorted demonic voice sounded on the recording.** What was said was so distorted, that it was impossible to make out, except for the last couple of words. I don't believe the voice was English, however, we had disputes amongst our members. Members of our team claim to have heard **"get cha (get ya)"** at the end of the distorted voice, however, I don't believe at all it was English. I don't know what language it was, but to me it sounded more like an H. Perhaps **"…hencha."** I think sometimes we make the mistake that everything we encounter is going to contain the English language, so we end up creating English words out of words that could be any language. I believe this was some sort of demonic language. News that came out a few weeks later might have solidified that assumption…

Further investigation brought us to the second floor. Several patient rooms were on the second floor. We went into most of them individually, listening for sounds or feeling for cold spots. Most of the building seemed fairly quiet while we were there, besides the random knocks, which really could be anything.

We were collecting another EVP out in front of the reception desk on the second floor when all of a sudden we heard a high-pitched moan. Our friends Brad and Eron were separate from the rest of the group, so we assumed it might be them until we heard their voice coming out of another room not even in the same direction. "Did y'all hear that?" Eron asked. The moan sounded again. I froze and nearly lost my ability to breathe. Chills crawled up my spine, and we all looked at each other with our mouths wide open. Instead of running, we started towards the sound. "Are you okay?" The moan continued. "Can we help you?" The moan sounded again.

Gently we crept toward the sound hoping not to scare whatever it was off. Finally, we reached the room it was coming from and we peeked our head in. The moan sounded again, this time louder. We stepped in. "The window is cracked," one of us said. We all took a deep breath. Every time the wind would blow, the wind crept through the cracks, creating the high-pitched moan. Debunked.

It's disappointing when you think you have evidence that you end up debunking, but it is somewhat a sigh of relief at the same time, because we never really know what we are dealing with. It also brings a somewhat modest self-realization to the investigation. Although many things prove over and over to be paranormal, not everything is, and sometimes something like this moan is just what we need to become more skeptical of activity we get. This is why most of what is in this book are things that I am fully convinced are completely paranormal. Much of the activity we have gotten that I find questionable, I have left out of this book for the most part, aside from the comical stories such as this.

So, we continued the investigation, finally coming to the third floor. The third floor wasn't much different than the second—the same quietness, the same feel. We started on another EVP. This time, our friend Brad who is kind of a brash guy decided that he wanted to get aggressive with the spirits. I don't remember what all exactly was said, but Brad was yelling and being condescending in the recording. What I do remember is him saying to the spirits, "I'll kick your ass!" Upon review of the EVP, we found a reply. Immediately after Brad yells that he will kick its ass, **a voice rises from beneath his yelling. "Come on!" it said.**

Provoking spirits is not something we recommend. It's never really certain what kind of spirits you might encounter. We rarely ever get aggressive with spirits unless absolutely necessary, which probably then is still not necessary. If you piss something off enough, it may follow you home or even further oppress or possess you. It's dangerous enough to go into these places searching for things that we shouldn't be; antagonizing takes it giant steps further.

Other than this, we didn't get any more activity worth noting. Sometimes we get activity but dismiss it quickly, or sometimes we just simply miss it if it is very quiet. We don't intend to explore evidence that just isn't strong enough or can easily be dismissed or debunked as shuffling of feet or a whisper or voice amongst us we might have forgotten to log as human or ambient.

We went to Sardis hospital two more times with different groups. The activity wasn't as prominent as it was this particular time. Finally, the third time we went in there, the police interrupted our investigation midway, and we were forced to leave. We are unsure exactly why they interrupted us or why we were forced to leave. We even made them aware that we had permission by their chief. That wasn't enough for us to stay. The information we found out a few days later may have been a factor and would chill us to the core.

Days later we had come to find that a girl had gone into the hospital and had left possessed. The word was that a nearby ghost team had actually been called to do an exorcism on her. The ghost team that performed the exorcism and told us that they had the audio from the exorcism called our team. We met them at a nearby Starbucks and listened to the audio. To this day I'm still not sure what to think of the audio. I suppose she could've been really possessed, but like with anything else, if we aren't there, we can't attest to it. After listening, Chance and I discussed it, and both of us had our doubts, however, bystanders to the exorcism claim the girl was legitimately possessed and smelled of rotted meat. It is certainly possible, but the audio alone from people I didn't know very well was not enough to convince me. To me, the audio reeked of poor acting. We will never really know the truth behind it.

Although I don't believe the possession to be factual, I do believe there is a demonic entity lurking in the darkness of the

The Darkness Unveiled: Investigating the Hidden World

Sardis Hospital. Possessions are real and they happen, probably more often than we actually know. Just because you aren't a caricature of the film The Exorcist, bending your back, flailing around, and projectile vomiting, doesn't mean you aren't possessed. There are people in every day life that do evil things that could potentially be possessed.

This building could easily be dismissed as just another building that has just bit the dust, but there is so much more to the North Panola Hospital. Since they closed it up, several famous paranormal teams have wanted to investigate this hospital, however, were denied. The town of Sardis, MS wants to put any speculation of anything paranormal or demonic residing in the hospital to rest, and perhaps that might be the best move if this possession really happened. However they may try to hide it, Sardis, zip code number **38666** will forever possess a dark entity within the hospital walls.

Morgue where we obtained demonic EVP with small orb middle-right

Hallway

The Darkness Unveiled: Investigating the Hidden World

Debris on the first floor

Creepy looking boiler room with orbs

Chance collecting an EVP with orb just in front of the recorder

The Darkness Unveiled: Investigating the Hidden World

a few orbs down the hall

Cemetery Investigations

Amongst the headstones, chiseled to memorialize those that have gone—some tragically, some naturally—spirits wander aimlessly and confused. There's something about the stillness and the coolness of cemeteries that although a little creepy at times, is somewhat soothing. I used to live right across from a cemetery on the backside of a church. My family had a pretty large front yard, so there was distance between our house and the cemetery, but still in my room from the second story of my house, I would peer out to see the headstones through the chain link fence. The soft glow from the church's only streetlight feathering just beyond the gate created shadows that would send shivers down my spine. Sometimes I would look out my window and scare myself from focusing far too long. Part of me liked being scared like a game of tag, knowing that as soon as I tagged it, it would chase me down until it tagged me back.

Cemeteries were easiest to investigate. Being that they were open to the public, Chance, Mel, and I could go at anytime we were strapped for a place to hunt; and we did—often. There was no need to get permission or notify that we were in there, we just went. No one would approach or bother us, because let's be real, who besides us is willing to wander around a cemetery after hours?

One of the downsides of cemetery investigations is the ambient noise. This is season dependant, however. During the fall and winter months, there is very little ambient noise that will disturb you aside from the wind and cracking and creaking trees. The spring and summer months create a number of obstructions. Every known creature from birds to insects is screaming and rustling around. Despite all of this, we still have successful investigations; it just makes it a little bit harder.

We have been in super haunted cemeteries and cemeteries that are so still and silent that you could hear a pin drop. Sometimes our audio recordings are laced with numerous voices and our pictures rampant with orbs and mists; sometimes there are no orbs or mists and pure silence on the recording. Like with any other investigation, we have activity one day and another day we will come back and there will be nothing. Several times the activity has been pretty overwhelming.

Randy Tatum

One cemetery we visited we felt like we hit a goldmine. There was only one problem: it was in the ghetto. It was a tiny cemetery that had a lot of buzz about it. They called it Old Raleigh Cemetery, and when we went there, the fear in us wasn't of the spirits. When we parked down the small dark road we did a lot of looking over our shoulders; we prayed we wouldn't get mugged. At that investigation almost the entire recording we got seemed to have voices on it, almost as if it was radio interference—which could have been the case. None of the words could be made out, but there seemed to be **constant whispering** that we couldn't make out. At the same investigation Chance and I are fairly sure we saw an apparition. While we were collecting EVP recordings both of us saw **a tall dark figure in the woods that disappeared** as we moved toward it. Could it have been human? Sure. If it was, that is far more terrifying than it being a ghost. Fortunately, we weren't attacked. Old Raleigh's activity seemed to dwindle upon future investigations, and to be quite honest, we never got anything solid enough to boast about.

An interesting experience happened at a cemetery that was conveniently located right beside an interstate. Can you hear my sarcasm? Although it was extremely loud compared to most cemeteries, our results weren't affected. When we walked through the gate, we could feel the energy. There was no wind, but right as we were doing our first EVP I had **dust kicked up on me**. None of us had moved, so it couldn't have been anyone besides something that wasn't visible.

Soon after during an EVP session, Chance asked if whatever was there could repeat the word "yellow." He also asked if the spirit would repeat the word "monopoly" just so it would be far more distinguishable than "yellow," which might sound more like "hello." When we reviewed the EVP we had an amazing response. **On both questions the spirit responded with exactly what we had asked and promptly—"Mo-no-po-ly" and "Yellow" were undeniably the intelligent response.** It was amazing. To have a spirit repeat the exact words you request it to in an EVP completely lacks any type of randomness. There is definitely tons of energy within this cemetery. Similarly, at another cemetery, we asked for a spirit's favorite color, and we received **"I-don't-have-a-co-lor" very quickly said.**

There is something evil at the Fog Rd cemetery. An EVP we obtained was very disturbing and chilling. Chance said, "All I need to know is your secrets, that's all I need to do. I just want to know what it is on that side—what you're going through. I want to help you if I can—various things like that. That's all." The response was clear and plain **"Well, kill yourself," is what the spirit angrily said.** This wasn't the only EVP we received at the Fog Road Cemetery, but it's unquestionably the most remarkable.

It's difficult to know exactly what to expect when going into any haunted place or potentially haunted place. A place such as a cemetery seems like an obvious place to go to communicate with what has been most closely associated with the dead, but sometimes you absolutely get nothing there; then, other times, at every turn there is a voice or goose bumps that trail up your arms and neck. Aside from speculative theories no one really knows why places are extremely active sometimes and completely dormant other times. All I can say is most of the time when you go and seek these things out, you are sure to get some type of response. Much of the time the response is there, but hard or impossible to hear—if the spirits are unable to gather up enough energy or if the ambient conditions do not comply.

A Germantown, Tennessee cemetery we visited was a pretty interesting experience. We were walking around with the recorder on asking questions as usual as Melissa was snapping pictures. Every time she snapped a picture, it was obvious on the recorder. She would move and snap in a different direction and so on. Finally, she turned one way and snapped a picture. Promptly after the picture was snapped, **a loud, demonic-sounding voice** that almost sounded just like a creature from the movie Gremlins came through. It said, clearly and unmistakably, **"Bright Light!"** It sounds a little unreal and just like something from a movie, but honest to God, it was unmistakable.

One other cemetery that we frequented, we had been there for a while collecting audio. We asked what its name was. It said **"Hiram"** which is a pretty strange name to get. Going through more audio we happened up on another EVP of a female saying her name was **"Tabatha,"** so on a future investigation, we just happened to look down at a gravestone and it was a double-named stone of a husband and wife. The first name on it was Hiram, the second name…well, it was Tabatha. That was very interesting.

Other obvious, easy to hear EVPs we got include: **"Fear the Dead"** in a Russian accent, **"Get out mother fuckers,"** several different names of people, **"I wasn't," "hot,"** when we asked how the spirit felt, **"Sadness,"** and several more, and these are just the ones we have on demand to listen to. There have been several EVPs—really good ones to our disadvantage—that are lost in hours of recordings, thus nearly impossible to find. Some of our stuff is saved on hard drives; others were never uploaded to a hard drive. It's just one of those things when you have more than twenty four hours worth of straight audio recordings, it's difficult to discover everything, as well as difficult to keep everything you do find within arm's length.

Audio recording, although a great way to collect evidence, can actually get kind of monotonous at times—partially because you cant always listen for the results immediately. So, in attempts at keeping our investigations free of tedium, we like to try new things. So, we figured a spirit might talk through a cell phone to us. Rather than creating feedback as we had during the Woodruff Fontaine House investigation, we decided to call one phone and leave it on a tombstone we believed to be an active area. We walked across the cemetery to start asking questions from the other phone. Although this seemed like a great idea, it produced no results at all. Yeah, I know it seemed like I was buttering you up for something good. It's important for me to note when an idea or investigation goes bust, because it's not always a swarm of activity. I want people to be aware of that, because if they were to try this and the first time produced no results, I don't want them to jump to conclusions that it is all fiction. I assure you, this is all very real.

Another experimentation we tried while recording, I reached my hand out and told whatever was there to touch my hand. I'll tell you, this was one of the most terrifying things I have done. Having been doing this for over a year, I had become pretty comfortable with investigating, but something like this definitely takes you right out of your comfort zone when you know there is probably something there. So, I reached out my hand. "If you are there, could you grab my hand?" I'm willing to admit that this may have been fear that made me believe that a spirit was touching my hand, but I can say with all sincerity **I believe a spirit did grab my hand.** It could have been my subconscious, but a picture taken during this exchange suggests otherwise. You be the judge. As you can see in the picture, there is an orb right on my hand.

The Darkness Unveiled: Investigating the Hidden World

We had cops come out to a cemetery once and shine lights on us. It was a pretty large group of us on this occasion. When we came out, he asked what we were doing. We thought for sure we were in trouble. So, we were honest with him and told him we were hunting ghosts, and he said the neighbors had called and said someone was in the cemetery. After talking to him and telling them about certain results we had gotten, he let us stay. I thought for sure he'd make us leave.

On cemetery investigations I seriously have no clue how many EVPs we have gotten. I couldn't possibly list all of them. The overwhelming amount of audio we have received isn't something we can put a number on, especially when referring to our cemetery investigations. This book is only highlights of a large, extreme adventure of a few years that Chance, Mel, and I all partook in that produced and made things real that have been denied and pushed aside for years.

Where I had dust kicked up on me.

The Darkness Unveiled: Investigating the Hidden World

Orb just above the recorder as we are asking questions

Same orb a few minutes after, only it moved just over Chance's head.

Huge, bright orb I captured in Elmwood (I believe)

Orbs

When dealing with orbs, you can't assume it's paranormal if you snap a shot that has one or many in it. It is widely known and regarded that dust particles can produce orb-like images. Although that is true, all orbs can't be discounted. There are significant orbs that may indeed be paranormal. There is certain criterion of orbs that you can dismiss and some that you may want to take a second look at. If you are looking for some sort of exact science behind it, I'm not sure you will find it.

Usually if there are tons of orbs in one picture, it's more likely that what you are seeing are dust particles. That's not to say that none of the orbs in the picture are paranormal, but it becomes a little easier to look past at that point. In my experience at looking at orbs, I tend to think the more electrical looking the orb is, the more likely it is spiritual. There have been some pictures we have taken in the past where you can actually see a face in the orb if you zoom in very closely. We believe those to be something worth taking a closer look.

We have gotten all kinds of orbs. A large percentage we tend to look past, not necessarily that they aren't paranormal, but because orbs just are on the bottom tier of evidence—at least, in my opinion. They are just far too unreliable to boast about as significant evidence. The only time we give any attention to the glowing balls, is if we do see a face in it or if we are conducting an EVP and the only orb in the picture is right in front of the recorder. Ghost hunting groups that pay too much attention to orbs are wasting their time in my opinion. There are far too many other directions you can go into for investigation to worry with glowing balls that sometimes are hard to tell if they are even spirits.

The Darkness Unveiled: Investigating the Hidden World

Randy Tatum

Effects of Ghost Hunting

Leaving a haunted place doesn't always mean the place leaves you. Having spirits follow you home is not a pleasant thing to have happen. It does however happen. I have had a few follow me home. From the rummaging across the room, to the taps on the wall, I assure you it wasn't mice.

There were nights that I had every light cut on in my house and I was going from room to room reading from my Bible trying to exorcise whatever was there. It sounds insane, but it happened. Sometimes I was prevented from sleeping by spirits in my room, wandering around and tapping on walls. Could some of it been me convincing myself that they were there? I'm not really sure. What I do know is that there were definitely times they were there.

Around the time when we first had started ghost hunting, I woke up one morning and came downstairs. This was when I was still living with my parents. I grabbed breakfast and coffee and started to head back upstairs. I heard my dad say, "Hey, R.T." (R.T. is my family name) "Yeah?" I asked, mid-step toward the upstairs. "Did you go ghost hunting last night by any chance?" he asked. "Well, yeah, why?" He replied, "I think something followed you home."

I was pretty shocked to hear my dad say this, so I stood there pretty frozen. He ended up explaining to me that while he was sleeping he heard someone yell at him very loudly. Whatever was there said **"Hey!"** really loud, which shot him up from his slumber. Could it have been a dream that had awoken him? Maybe. However, I think if he really believed it was a dream he wouldn't have even mentioned it. To even bring up and ask if I had been ghost hunting when I actually had been ghost hunting was significant enough.

After that situation, I was pretty cognitive of my surroundings—perhaps a little too cognitive. I started peering at everything in my house with a magnifying glass, therefore, basically everything that happened in the house, I freaked out. The icemaker would pop, and I would jump. No matter what it was, I was convinced it was paranormal. Most of it wasn't paranormal, of course, but it really made me more aware of my surroundings knowing that something really was in my house.

You can make fun of me if you want, but to this day, I sleep with some form of light on. Yeah, I get it, I'm like a five year old—whatever; when you have gone through and experienced what I have experienced, you can't ignore the dark. When you are completely aware that something lurks within the shadows, does pitch black really create the most comfortable environment for sleeping? Not for me. Fortunately for me, my wife is a good sport in this, and she doesn't complain about a light being on.

Not only would the spirits follow us home on occasion, sometimes we would get extremely drained from an investigation. Spirits acquire energy from electronics and our bodies in order to speak or manifest to us. Sometimes our batteries from our camera or our flashlights might get dim and the brand new batteries would need replacing. Other times our bodies would be what the spirits used, and sometimes this would leave us just absolutely dead. You could argue that it might have been the crash from the caffeine we had slammed before every hunt or that it was just the fact that we didn't get home many days until two a.m., but to me, it was different than a crash or just being tired; my body would feel just weighted.

Many times I would come back from a hunt depressed or anxious. Could there have been other factors at play? Of course. I wont say there wasn't a reason other than being affected by spirits, but I do believe much of the depression and anxiety were a direct oppression from the demonic. It's scary to think about, and I wish it were wrong, but I'm pretty sure it was a demon oppressing me. I wasn't the only one who had draining effects, however, I can't attest for the other's depression or anxiety.

The effects of demons and spirits can be easily dismissed as something else—such as some evil image that randomly pops in your head you may feel is just random. It's easy to convince yourself whatever your oppression is whether drowsiness, anger, depression, irritability, or anything really, that it is only yourself and *your* psyche. Be aware, that is not always the case. Sometimes those things we can't see are looking for a way to use us—sometimes even abuse us.

Randy Tatum

Theories

Eventually we all need to get to a point when we realize that there is something there that we can't see. We are not alone no matter how much we try to convince ourselves. Forget about the 'mean tricks' your parents played on you in telling you there was an Easter Bunny or a Tooth Fairy and discover that the things you can't see or don't know anything about aren't always mythology or folklore. There is something that exists beyond what we can touch and see. Sometimes it may leak into our reality and we shrug it off, because we take a second glance and it's not there. "My eyes are playing tricks on me," we will say. To some of us nothing may ever manifest or some of these same people may not seek it out, and that is perfectly fine (I suggest not ever seeking it out.) However, what I do want is that everyone get to a point where they believe, because this isn't at all mythology—far from it. From there, it is important that you discover what it all means.

There are times still where I am sitting on the couch and I'll see a shadow or hear a noise, and still, my 'rational human mind' thinks that it's nothing or it's just a cloud going over the sun. I am constantly trying to convince myself what I see is not what I see. Maybe we *should* just shrug these things off. It might be a good idea that we not entertain these images, because the more I give these things attention, the more frequently they seem to prod at me. We MUST know that they are there, though.

I have theories surrounding what we are coming in contact with. Some may disagree, some may find it intriguing—I just hope that those that look at this evidence formulate some opinion on it. This stuff isn't just some random frequencies or our minds playing tricks on us. All of this is very real and very alive and quite frankly anywhere and everywhere—not just in haunted hotels or cemeteries.

Aside from fire, the Bible describes Hell as eternal separation from God and his angels. Here on earth, sometimes we are connected to God through people. We may have a situation that happens that really makes us see the good in people or make us want to be a better person. We may have a religious experience that we know is some kind of miracle or revelation. Other times, we may pray and have comfort or answers. So, in a sense, here on Earth, we are connected to God, although sometimes we may not feel it, but what about these spirits we are encountering?

While some people look at haunts and immediately say that they are just ghosts roaming the Earth, I look at them and wonder immediately why? I wonder why they are here, why they seem to not communicate in a way that we are aware what they are or why they are here, why they are in some places and not in others—all these questions come to mind with no clear answer. So, focusing in on all these questions, the mystery strengthens. For this very reason, I am almost entirely convinced that most of what we are dealing with is somewhat of a Hell on Earth. We have always looked up as a symbol to Heaven and looked down as a symbol of Hell, but in

The Darkness Unveiled: Investigating the Hidden World

reality both may be right in front of our faces on a different plane of existence. Perhaps we are tapping into exactly Hell and communicating with demons and/or people who have passed and gone to Hell. If Hell were truly separation from God and His angels, wouldn't being in limbo, seeing people move around and live their lives and not being able to interact or have any of the mutual emotions we have here on Earth such as love. To not be able to interact with people who are made in the image of God or not being able to interact with God or have a religious experience of any kind; rather being bound to the chains of the Devil barely being able to speak, and when you do speak, you aren't able to say what you want to say or be saved by anyone.

Imagine you die and all you have left is your past regret. Envision that you can see people around you living their lives doing the same things you are doing, making the same mistakes you are making. Opening your mouth, you feel your vocal chords vibrate, but a dark hand comes over your face and now nothing more than a breath comes out. You want to so bad tell that person that you made a mistake and to not make the same. The mysteries of the universe are finally yours, but you are unable to tell anyone that there is a God or that you are bound by the demonic. Think of how awful that image is. I think of this when we ghost hunt—that these people might be trying to reveal to us what they know, but the demons only allow words to bleed through that will make no sense to the living. I imagine a sea of lost people, each one guarded by his or her own demon.

I know, anyone that may be reading this book that isn't religious, I'm getting eye rolls. I understand, however, it's got to be something, and in the decades of paranormal investigations, we seem to never have any further revelation that these are just people's spirits wandering around. At some point I feel if these were just ghosts wandering around, we would know a lot more about them. But it seems like these spirits are prevented from telling us anything we want or need to know. It seems they are sworn to secrecy or amongst us just to confuse us.

Some ghost hunters pretend like they have made a lot of progress with spiritual investigation. To a degree they have. For instance, it's not even debatable any longer that these things exist. You may have different opinions on what they are, but to completely deny it now is pure ignorance. But these hunters pretend that they have made progress that has them on the brink of determining exactly what these things are and how to help them. The truth is, we never will have anything rock solid. That doesn't mean it's incorrect to pursue, but I wouldn't go in it with complete optimism. No matter what progress is made, there are always going to be gaps, because our understanding and God's understanding are two completely different realities. When we think we have it on lock, we should keep digging.

The Darkness Unveiled: Investigating the Hidden World

One might ask, "if demons and people in hell manifest, then why don't we see God and angels manifest?" There's actually an easy answer to that. They do, over and over. The problem with the human psyche is that we are bent to recognize the negative and evil before recognizing the good. Bad has a tendency to overshadow good. For instance, when our car breaks down, we scream at the sky at how awful our lives are and how unlucky we are, but we forget the reason our car broke down is because we actually have a car. Not only that, but the car we have hasn't broken down in several years. We take a lot of things that happen in our lives for granted—just like we take for granted the proof of God that we wake up to everyday. From the function of our bodies, to the rise of the sun, God is manifesting in ways that to us are just the normalcy of everyday life. So, maybe why we don't see God manifest before us is possibly because God and demons manifest themselves differently. Just because we can record demons and spirits, doesn't mean we can record God. Our blessings are abundant; our eyes, however, are devious.

So, in my opinion, what we are tapping into isn't just some dead people roaming around in a mist or an orb; we are tapping into an entirely different realm, which I believe is Hell. From the demonic recordings we have gotten, to the subtle speak we hear from these spirits, I don't really see what else it could be. Perhaps, I'm a little biased being that I am a Christian, so maybe I'm bent to think this way. But, think about it! If you spend even a moment thinking about it, it's impossible to not involve some sort of religiosity with any of this I'm speaking about.

These spirits are unable to communicate with the living, intervene in anything going on around them, help others understand the mysteries which we all seek, and unable to change their situation in anyway. So, this hell they are dwelling in, is their limbo, separate from God and people. Demons on the other hand have the power to have a real effect on the outside world. These spirits and demons are on the same plane of existence, which is why we make contact with both. If you think what I'm saying is wrong, offer me a different theory that doesn't sound far-fetched. I see a lot of people unwilling to acknowledge God or demons, but quick to run to left field to start talking serious about some kind of matrix we live in—that we all are just brains in a tank and nothing we touch or see is real in any way. Think rationally about this stuff and really analyze what this all could mean. Don't just go out in left field and create your own sci-fi movie.

What we know as 'rational,' really spirits don't even fit into that picture. Yet, here they are amongst us every day. We can't ignore that. So, we must try and think rationally about something so irrational. It sounds almost contradictory, but there is rationality in all of this irrationality—we can't just say, "Well, ghosts exist, so nothing is off the table." If we go to those lengths then we really are just creating our own horror movie. We should take what we do know or have been taught and see how it really matches up with what is being revealed to us. We may have thought our entire lives that demons are a myth, but yet, here are things that we are coming in contact with that seem to project the same caricatures of so called 'fictional' demons.

I can't begin to know everything about the hidden world we pass by every day, but I can speculate rationally. If you are a person who is bitter by religion or think its all-just make believe, I get it. There's a lot about religion to be angry about—from the priests molesting children to the hypocrites, but just know that none of that is the embodiment of God. Know that the other realms do bleed into our own, and when evil things like this happen it's likely involving the demonic. For the people that think it's all make believe, I'm just not sure I would ever be able to convince you that it's not. One of the reasons I wrote this book is to present you with some facts. It's up to you to formulate your own theories or tag onto mine. I just urge you to look at the evidence we have collected and do some soul searching.

Something Good

I can't just make a blanket statement about God revealing Himself over and over again without actually giving you a little proof of that. I also don't want this to be a book just focused on the negative spirit world. There is a positive spirit world. So, I'll tell you a story that was obviously God reminding me He is still there.

I was driving, listening to some music very loud when all of a sudden my steering wheel began to feel heavy and was vibrating. I looked down at my gages only to find the low air light on. Immediately I knew that I had a flat on my fairly new tire. So, I pulled over in the hot sun. That particular day was supposed have a heat index of 106 degrees. As soon as I step out, I feel the sun beating down on my face. Sweat poured immediately from my pores. I had only a little water left. Changing tires isn't a big deal to me usually. I'm actually very quick with it, so I wasn't concerned—I'd be done in five minutes. (I thought wrong). While jacking up the car with my awful scissor car jack, the rod started to bend, making it almost impossible to turn. Finally, my car started to roll because I had forgotten to set the parking brake. At this time, I heard a truck pulling up behind me. As I look up, the car rolled back and the jack fell out from under it, sending the rotor crashing to the ground, only dampened by my tire being partially under it.

"You need some help," I heard. Pouring sweat, I say, "Yeah, actually I do. I just had the jack fall. The guy comes up and tries to help me, but there is no space for the jack to even fit under the car. "I'll go home and get my dad's jack. He has a good one." So, he left. At this point, a ten-minute job is now going on twenty minutes, and we still aren't anywhere near to finishing. Not even two minutes later another man pulls up and asks if I need help. Not entirely sure how long the other guy will take to come back, I accept the man's help. He winds up having a three-ton jack, and with a little ingenuity we finally completed the job. I thanked the guy. He said, "I'm thankful that God gave me the opportunity to help someone today. The only thing I ask of you is that you pass on the blessing." I assured the guy I would.

So, I started back out on the road on my donut. I get not even two miles down the road, and there is a man walking with the sun beating down and sweating profusely. He was at the end of the ramp to get on the highway, so I didn't even have enough time to build up speed. God made it easy for me. Picking up hitchers isn't something I do, but in order to keep my word to the man that just helped me, I picked the guy up. The man proceeded to tell me where he was going, which was almost exactly where I was going. He told me that he was trying to at least make it to the next gas station, which was a few miles down the road and that he wasn't sure if he was going to make it because he had just ran out of water.

I don't know whether the man would've died of heat exhaustion if I hadn't picked him up or not, however, I do know that if the chain of events that happened didn't happen exactly how they did, I might have never picked up the guy. There was something at work there, and I believe it was straight from God.

Anyone can talk their selves into thinking this is some kind of coincidence, but these kind of things happen and *have* happened to me many times. We just forget. It is sad we forget, but we do. When I dropped the man off, I told him the same thing the man who had helped me, told me—to 'pass on a blessing.' I hope he continued the chain. I will never know how far that first act transferred, but if you keep your eyes open, God may give you a situation and make it so easy for you to do something good. How you respond is up to you. Sometimes it may not even be about the situation. It may be something your heart needs to replenish your faith.

Conclusion

When I think about every piece of evidence we have collected over the years, I'm reminded of a story the late pastor Adrian Rogers spoke about. He said he was on a plane and was speaking to a very intelligent man whom professed to be an atheist. He asked the man if he thought he knew 90% of everything there was to know. The man of course replied with "of course not." He asked if he knew 70% of everything there was to know. The man of course replied with "of course not." He finally got to 30%, and the man replied, "I might know 30%." Pastor Rogers asked him, "Well, do you think God could fit anywhere in that 70% that you don't know?"

We all seem to think we have it figured out, but we likely know less than the man who claimed he knew only 30% of everything there is to know. Still, when something that we can't see or can't feel is being discussed, there are some quick to scoff and treat us as if we are crazy for entertaining the idea. Here I am, not only believing but also actually having proof available on demand that something beyond physical exists, and still there are some that refuse to even humor a listen. Even renowned so-called scientists who haven't even investigated these things deny they exist to those who have actually been out in the field and studied this. There is a trend—most of the people I know or have heard that refuse to believe this stuff usually have very large egos. Arrogance and disbelief are very synonymous for the very reason that these people don't want to be duped, and they are well aware that no one will ever really know. So, they can beat their chests that they have all the answers, which ultimately in reality boil down to *no* answers.

The age we are living in, trust me, I understand skepticism. Believing in something that has been published on the cover of the National Enquirer our entire lives—especially in the age of 'fake news'—is not easy to do. No one wants to be duped. I am one of the kings of skepticism and distrust. But how anyone can argue with actual evidence is beyond me. It's obvious to me now, and I hope this book has taken you one step closer to it being obvious to you as well. I used to not care a whole heck of a lot if people believed any of our ghost hunting stories, but I've come to a point where I believe it is extremely crucial that people believe these stories. This isn't just some make believe world that you can look at for a couple of seconds and then go on with your life. This world we are living in is not just flesh and bone; there is so much that we don't understand working behind the scenes.

It seems insane to believe such a thing, believe me, I know. To be holding a recorder out into the air and asking questions to what seems like nothing makes you feel like a schizophrenic. At least, until that voice manifests on the recorder, and then you realize that we really aren't alone. It gives me the chills sometimes to think that if I walk down the street something could be walking with me, if I go into the bathroom, something could be walking with me; it doesn't matter where we go, something could be there and we not realize it.

This book is not meant to scare; that is far from my intent. I only want people to step outside of their comfort zone. I urge whoever is reading this to look intently at this stuff, because it *does* matter. Just because we can't see something, doesn't mean that it is irrelevant, conversely, it might actually mean that it is the *most* relevant. Some people think after you die there is nothing and that God and the Devil are merely figments of our imagination, or that Hell is a made up place that was created just to strike fear in us so we would behave. I don't believe that is the case at all. In reality there is a battle for our minds. Our soul is constantly being chipped away and the wound is persistently trying to mend. We either can help it to mend or we can continue to let it whittle away until we are nothing.

Death and the afterlife are probably the most immensely sought out mysteries in everyone's mind. Most people are fearful of death, because we really don't know exactly what to expect. This evidence proves that it doesn't just go pitch black when we die, but that in some way we live on and that there is a battle behind the scenes of what we know as reality. Unless you are willing to put some grand twist on these results and say that maybe they are aliens, or we are formulating these sentences in our brain and telepathically manifesting them on the recorder subconsciously, or it's some alternate dimension that is going about life at the same time as we are and we are tapping into it, then we must look to this as something spiritual. (Why do these seem logical but spirits aren't?)

Most importantly, when we come to the realization that this is spiritual, we have to do some soul searching, and we must do something with the information revealed. For me, it was being more spiritually aware and gripping tighter to God. I was already a Christian before I started ghost hunting, but the results we found only strengthened the cement. To some, this will have the inverse effect—and it *has* had the inverse effect on people I know. I will never understand why, but that is their journey, not mine. All I can do is reiterate my experiences and tell you what effect it has had on me and hope that you come to the same conclusion as me.

Everyone always wants proof to believe in anything. I can't give you God on a platter. God is too complex for that. I can, however, give you our experiences with unseen forces, as I have. Can you simultaneously believe in these forces and then completely deny the existence of God? Now that you see that the invisible is possible, can you at least put God in the 'maybe' category? If you cant there is a huge fallacy in your thinking. This stuff should blow your mind and result in some kind of religious journey. The invisible is possible as this book makes clear, so why is God so hard to believe?

To never write this book is to hide a reality that others may take for granted or never come to know. All I know is that the mysteries of the universe are important. We may only know the physical world, but it is subtlety and the things that aren't so obvious that are most important. If you have never searched, I hope this is the start of your search; if you have searched and never found, I hope this book helps you to find some direction. What we feel and what we see isn't all there is in this world. It isn't even a drop in the bucket. We can't begin to fathom what truths are hidden, but apathy and negativity isn't the direction we should go. Only with open-mindedness and careful examination can we begin to learn things we don't know.

If you are still reading this book and have decided this is just a bunch of rubbish or that I'm full of it, I can't convey to you how extremely wrong you are. If you are reading this and know I'm telling the truth and that there is something to this and you decide to do nothing with it, deciding to ignore it may be more disastrous than you think. With spirits absolutely existing, we should take religion very seriously. I don't believe this life is about making more money than the next or being more successful or even exclusively just loving one another. This life is about discovery—the loving one another and being successful may trail along with it, but finding out what this life is actually about and finding our purpose is the most important. Until we come to that conclusion, we are simply what we are hunting—wandering and aimless ghosts.

If you would like to see some additional pictures and hear some of the EVPs discussed in this book, visit our crew's Facebook page at: www.facebook.com/DarknessUnveiledParanormalInvestigators/

If you'd like to see some of the videos I refer to in this book, search for **"Woodruff-Fontaine Paranormal Investigation"** or **"Bryce Mental Institution sounds caught on tape"**

Acknowledgements

I would like to thank God for the life he has given me and for the people He has placed in my life. Thanks to my wife for all her support, encouragement and love. My family for everything you have done—my Mom specifically for reading all of my books and giving her feedback, edits and time. Thanks to Chance and Mel—not for you guys and our experiences, this book wouldn't exist, and I'm glad that we all became good friends. To anyone that joined us on a ghost hunt, specifically my friends Eron, Duane, Scott, Eddie, and anyone else that may have joined us—thank you. Another thanks goes to Melissa for the work on my past book covers and for allowing me to use the pictures you took for this book. If you read this book, thank you as well.

Made in the USA
Columbia, SC
11 September 2018